EXTREME SPORTS EVENTS

IRONMAN TRIATHLONS

ETHAN OLSON

SportsZone
An Imprint of Abdo Publishing
abdobooks.com

abdobooks.com

Published by Abdo Publishing, a division of ABDO, PO Box 398166, Minneapolis, Minnesota 55439. Copyright © 2024 by Abdo Consulting Group, Inc. International copyrights reserved in all countries. No part of this book may be reproduced in any form without written permission from the publisher. SportsZone™ is a trademark and logo of Abdo Publishing.

Printed in the United States of America, North Mankato, Minnesota.
102023
012024

THIS BOOK CONTAINS RECYCLED MATERIALS

Cover Photo: Sean M. Haffey/Getty Images for Ironman/Getty Images Sport/Getty Images
Interior Photos: Nils Nilsen/Getty Images for Ironman/Getty Images Sport/Getty Images, 5; Alex Grimm/Getty Images Sport/Getty Images, 6; Red Line Editorial, 9; Tom Pennington/Getty Images for Ironman/Getty Images Sport/Getty Images, 10–11, 12–13, 23, 28; Marco Garcia/AP Images, 15; Ezra Shaw/Getty Images for Ironman/Getty Images Sport/Getty Images, 16; Gonzalo Arroyo Moreno/Getty Images for Ironman/Getty Images Sport/Getty Images, 18–19; Ryan Sosna-Bowd/Getty Images Sport/Getty Images, 20; Bryn Lennon/Getty Images for Ironman/Getty Images Sport/Getty Images, 24–25; Charlie Crowhurst/Getty Images for Ironman/Getty Images Sport/Getty Images, 27

Editors: Charlie Beattie and Steph Giedd
Series Designer: Cynthia Della-Rovere

Library of Congress Control Number: 2023939475

Publisher's Cataloging-in-Publication Data

Names: Olson, Ethan, author.
Title: Ironman Triathlons / by Ethan Olson
Description: Minneapolis, Minnesota: Abdo Publishing, 2024 | Series: Extreme sports events | Includes online resources and index.
Identifiers: ISBN 9781098292379 (lib. bdg.) | ISBN 9798384910312 (ebook)
Subjects: LCSH: Extreme sports--Juvenile literature. | Action sports (Extreme sports)--Juvenile literature. | Ironman triathlons--Juvenile literature. | Triathlon--Juvenile literature. | Running races--Juvenile literature. | Swimming--Juvenile literature. | All terrain bicycling--Juvenile literature.
Classification: DDC 796.046--dc23

TABLE OF CONTENTS

CHAPTER 1
Shattering Records **4**

CHAPTER 2
Training for an
Ironman Triathlon **10**

CHAPTER 3
Mastering Endurance **18**

CHAPTER 4
Becoming an Ironman **24**

Glossary 30
More Information 31
Online Resources 31
Index 32
About the Author 32

CHAPTER 1

SHATTERING RECORDS

The first two stages of the 2014 Ironman World Championship hadn't gone as Mirinda Carfrae thought they would. After finishing the swimming and cycling portions, Carfrae was 14 minutes, 30 seconds behind the race leader, Daniela Ryf. Though Ryf was new to the Ironman World Championship, she was a two-time Olympian. Ryf was also the top finisher in her Ironman races in Switzerland and Denmark that year. That was how she had qualified for the Ironman World Championship in Kona, Hawaii. But Carfrae was a two-time Ironman world champion. She knew what it took to win the grueling competition.

Australia's Mirinda Carfrae finished on the podium six times in seven Ironman World Championship competitions, including three victories.

Carfrae's comeback in the 2014 World Championship was still a record when she retired from competition in 2023.

Carfrae swiftly transitioned off her bicycle. She was determined to catch up to Ryf on foot. Carfrae showed no signs of slowing down despite having already traveled 114.4 miles (184.1 km) during the swimming and cycling portions. She still had 26.2 miles in which to catch up. Carfrae used her long strides to move quickly through the tropical heat. She was breathing heavily, but she kept pushing and slowly closed the gap.

Eight hours and 34 minutes into the race, Carfrae was right behind Ryf. It was Carfrae's time to go for the lead. She picked up her pace and zipped into first place.

With only a few miles to go, it was time for Carfrae to give everything her body had left.

As she crossed the finish line, Carfrae grabbed the Ironman banner and lifted it above her head while letting out a cheer. She had just pulled off the largest comeback in Ironman World Championship history.

TOUGHEST IN THE WORLD

The Ironman Triathlon World Championship is a triathlon event held annually in Kona, Hawaii, on Hawaii's biggest island. The competition was first held on another Hawaiian island, Oahu, in 1978. But in 1981 the event moved to Kona, where it became recognized as one of the biggest racing challenges in the world.

The race also became popular. Soon the Ironman organization started holding more events around the world. By 2023 there were more than 170 races for athletes to compete in. These events are used as qualifiers for the limited spots in the World Championship. In 2023 the Ironman organization also changed its hosting tradition for the World Championship. The men's and women's championships are now split between Kona and Nice, France. In 2023 the men's competition was scheduled for Nice, while the women's was scheduled for Kona. The races were planned to rotate locations each year through 2026.

There are three portions of the Ironman triathlon—swimming for 2.4 miles (3.9 km), cycling for 112 miles (180.2 km), and running for 26.2 miles (42.2 km). Each portion also has cutoff times. This adds pressure to maintain a pace that will allow athletes to finish each section of the race in time.

The idea of the Ironman began with Judy and John Collins. The couple had competed in the 1974 Mission Bay Triathlon in San Diego, California. This was the first modern triathlon in the United States. After moving to Hawaii in 1975, the Collinses decided they wanted to start their own racing tradition. Their dream came true in 1978, when 15 men stepped up to the challenge for the first time. This race was different from other, more common triathlons, which are much shorter in distance for all three portions.

As time passed, participant numbers multiplied. By the 10th edition of the Ironman in 1987, there were 1,381 athletes who started the race. People from around the world wanted to test themselves in the grueling competition.

The race can seem like a never-ending grind. Racers jump straight out of the water to get on their bikes as quickly as possible. Then they face a similar transition between cycling and running. Meanwhile, the athletes must always be mindful of their pacing. The weather in Kona is

IRONMAN TRIATHLONS IN NORTH AMERICA

Ironman events are held around the world, including 12 full 140.6-mile (226.3-km) races in North America.

hot and humid. So it's key for athletes to plan out the best times to fuel their bodies during the race. An Ironman triathlon is both a mental and a physical battle that goes on for hours. But participants come back year after year, ready for the challenge.

CHAPTER 2

TRAINING FOR AN IRONMAN TRIATHLON

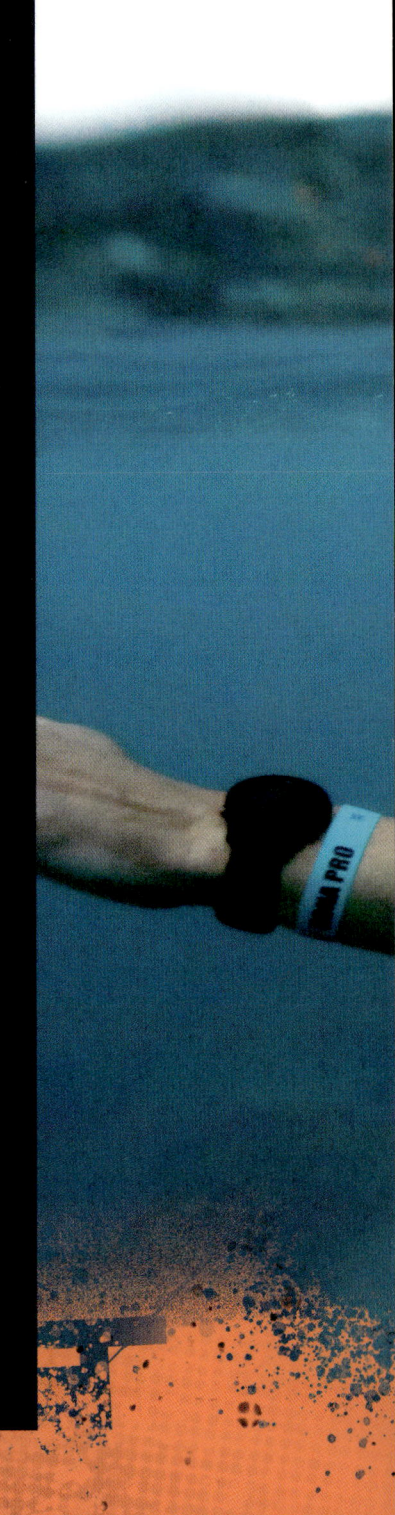

As with any triathlon, Ironman athletes must train themselves well in each of the race portions. Some athletes may already be stronger in certain aspects. But sticking to detailed training plans for each one is necessary for an athlete to be fully prepared.

People put in months, or even a full year, of training before taking on any Ironman triathlon. The Ironman organization recommends training for all portions at the same time, by mapping out days each week to train for each segment of the race. An athlete may spend one day focusing her time on cycling, and then work on swimming the following day. As the months go on, training becomes more intense. Over time, athletes

American Tim O'Donnell swims the first leg of the 2019 Ironman World Championship in Kona, Hawaii.

increase the distance of training sessions and the amount of time spent training.

Experienced triathletes plan multiple workouts per day. Sometimes those include brick workouts, which consist of training in two portions back-to-back. This helps athletes prepare for the immediate switches between swimming, cycling, and running.

It's common for people to train for cycling indoors on a stationary bike to practice at specific speeds. Training this way also means they do not have to stop for traffic, which

Racers bunch together in the water at the start of the 2016 Ironman World Championship.

is not present in the actual race. For swimming, many athletes train in pools. But it's important to spend time in open water as well. This helps swimmers understand the power of currents and how to maintain speed while the water pushes their bodies in different directions. For the running portion, some athletes prefer training on treadmills, while other athletes prefer running outside.

Competitors must be careful to avoid overtraining, which can cause injuries. They must also keep an eye on their mental preparation. Training for an Ironman takes an intense focus. It can be hard for some racers to balance their lives.

Athletes like two-time Ironman Rogeema Kenny can train 15 to 18 hours per week on top of work, school, and other parts of life. Kenny stayed motivated in part by the bonds she made with other Ironman athletes. Communicating with other athletes is a healthy way to stay motivated and feel a sense of belonging. Athletes share goals, training plans, and life experiences with each other. This helps them continue pushing through the difficult preparation for an Ironman event.

Nutrition is also important to consider, during both training and the race. Typically Ironman athletes increase their protein and carbohydrate intake while training. Protein is especially important. It helps the athletes' muscles and immune systems function and recover while training for, competing in, and recovering from this long, grueling race.

Including both the men's and women's divisions, the average Ironman finishing time is 12 hours and 49 minutes. The race never stops, so athletes must fuel their bodies while in motion. Each athlete can have a support crew to provide them small amounts of food and beverages while they race. Athletes typically consume more during their bike portion and much less in the running portion.

Some athletes drink Coca-Cola while racing because the sugar and caffeine can give them a boost of energy late in the race.

Planning around this is key to keeping a finish time as low as possible.

Lucy Charles-Barclay of the United Kingdom placed second in the Ironman World Championship four times between 2017 and 2022.

A GLOBAL CHALLENGE

Because Ironman triathlons are held in many countries, athletes also need to take the unique challenges of the race location into account. Climate and other conditions vary greatly. For example, the Ironman held in Brazil is hotter and more humid than the one held in Sweden, which has a milder climate. Athletes need to make sure their bodies are ready for challenges such as high temperatures or rough terrain.

Because so many people dream of competing in an Ironman, securing a spot in the race can be challenging. Registration typically opens a full year before the race date. Some of the 170-plus Ironman events around the world act as qualifiers for the World Championship in Kona, Hawaii, and Nice, France. Typically an athlete can qualify for the World Championship by earning a top-five finish in another Ironman event. Athletes can also qualify by winning their age group at the previous World Championship. Only a certain number of athletes are allowed to compete. For example, a total of approximately 5,000 spots were offered for the 2023 World Championship.

IRONKIDS

Kids from ages zero to 17 can participate in Ironman events as well with the Ironkids Fun Run. There is a Diaper Dash, which is a 26.2-foot (8-m) crawl for all ages. The Toddler Dot Trot is an 80-foot (24.4-m) race for kids ages one to three. The half-mile (0.8-km) race is for kids who are ages three to eight, and the one-mile (1.6-km) race is for ages five to 17.

CHAPTER 3

MASTERING ENDURANCE

There are several challenges that athletes face during an Ironman event. The swimming segment is particularly dangerous as athletes are at risk of drowning. For this reason, it's the first portion. Placing the swimming leg of the race first helps prevent athletes from overheating in the water and potentially drowning. But there is still the risk for possible heart issues, as the start of an Ironman race is highly stressful and athletes are pumping with adrenaline. During a race in 2023, one competitor suffered a heart attack during the swimming portion and died as a result.

Since all athletes in a division race at once, there's also the risk of people getting in each other's way, leading to injuries. This can happen

The swimming portion of the Ironman is always first so that racers have the most energy to complete it safely.

Racers must be careful to avoid others, especially during the cycling leg.

in any portion and is common while cycling. If one athlete rides too close to another, they can collide and cause a crash involving many others. This is why it is important for athletes to always stay alert while racing. In 2020 one Ironman competitor accidentally drifted into another while cycling. The two athletes piled up, causing a third to crash as well.

In the 2023 Ironman Texas event, Art Rascon crashed his bike into a barrel just eight miles (12.9 km) into the biking portion. Rascon broke both of his wrists. He was in so much pain that quitting the race seemed likely. "Those thoughts were passing through the mind. But then, there was me trying to prevail over those thoughts, saying 'I've got to do it. I can do this.'" With more than 100 miles (161 km) left to bike, and a marathon to run, Rascon pressed on. He was able to finish just under two hours before the finishing deadline.

FUELING UP

It takes great focus to complete an Ironman. Finding time to eat and drink during the race can be difficult.

CRAWLING TO THE FINISH

Julie Moss had an eight-minute lead over second place going into the final running stretch of the 1982 Ironman. However, Moss had pushed herself to the limit. Her legs began giving out with cramps. Moss collapsed several times, and people tried to help her up. She was able to crawl to the finish line. However, the runner in second place had caught up. Moss ended up finishing second by 29 seconds.

But it's important for all athletes to replace the salt and electrolytes lost from sweating to avoid cramping up during a race. Dehydration happens when a person does not drink enough fluids. It can cause athletes' arms and legs to feel weak. Athletes may even lose consciousness due to the fatigue and lack of water. This often happens when racers are running near the end of the race.

To avoid dehydration, athletes need to pay attention to how much water they drink during a race. Water stations tend to be available every 10 miles (16 km) during the cycling leg and every one or two miles (1.6 or 3.2 km) during the running portion. Drinking water before feeling thirsty can also help athletes keep their bodies fueled during the long hours of competing in an Ironman.

Though it's important to drink water, it's also crucial to not drink too much water. Doing so can lead to hyponatremia. A racer's body needs proper levels of salt and electrolytes. Racers who drink only water can become ill. In some extreme cases, lack of salt and electrolytes can lead to death. A study at an Ironman in Frankfurt, Germany, found that approximately 10 percent of finishers suffered from hyponatremia.

Medical professionals are placed throughout an Ironman race to offer help to athletes. It's common for athletes to struggle and not finish an Ironman. In most World Championships, 5 to 7 percent of athletes do not finish. Having professionals on the scene to offer help right away is crucial for keeping athletes safe.

Shaikh Nasser Bin Hamad Al Khalifa of Bahrain was one of the competitors to take part in the 2018 Ironman World Championship in Hawaii.

CHAPTER 4

BECOMING AN IRONMAN

Every Ironman athlete must pay a fee to enter an Ironman event. Those fees differ throughout different countries. However, top finishers in Ironman events earn cash prizes in addition to qualifying for the World Championship.

The biggest prize pool is offered at the Ironman World Championship. In 2022 the total $750,000 prize was split between the top 15 finishers. The men's winner, Norway's Gustav Iden, took home $125,000.

Finishing an Ironman World Championship is an incredible accomplishment. Those who reach the finish line are greeted by thousands of cheering fans, which can be overwhelming. In this moment, athletes can also feel the sensation known as "runner's high." This causes

Germany's Laura Philipp celebrates winning the 2019 Ironman 70.3 in Marbella, Spain.

strong emotions of joy, pride, and even pain relief. For this reason, athletes may not feel the physical effects of the race until hours later.

Some competitors struggle with their mental health after completing an Ironman. They've all spent months of their lives preparing for a single competition. Win or lose, finishing an Ironman can leave a void in an athlete's life. Athletes in the Ironman community refer to this as post-Ironman depression syndrome (PIDS). It can cause sadness or leave athletes wondering what they want to do with their lives. Rogeema Kenny said that after the race was over, she felt like "a rug had been pulled from underneath [her]." Once her sole focus was finished, she realized how PIDS affected her. To overcome it, she found that it really helped to talk to other Ironman triathletes about PIDS and share experiences. Talking about mental or physical struggles with others who

UNFINISHED BUSINESS

In 2005 Sarah Reinertsen had one of the most memorable finishes to an Ironman. She was trying to become the first-ever female amputee to finish the race. Reinertsen had tried the year before and crossed the finish line, only to learn she had missed the cycling cutoff time. She came back the next year. This time she met the mark. Reinertsen fell to the ground, crying in disbelief. Everyone around her went wild for her legendary finish.

Competitors enter the water at the 2019 Ironman Wales competition.

have gone through the same thing can help competitors understand what they are feeling.

Kenny also emphasized taking the necessary time to recover mentally and physically. The amount of time may vary from one competitor to another. Athletes must have a plan for recovery so that their muscles can heal properly. A person's muscles need two to three weeks of recovery following an Ironman. It can take longer to recover if the athlete suffered injuries or other problems during the race. Athletes shouldn't be hard on themselves if they need a break or don't feel ready to train again right away.

Kyle Pease, *left*, and his brother Brent compete together in the 2018 Ironman World Championship.

THE IRONMAN COMMUNITY

Once the right recovery is done, staying involved in the triathlon community can help athletes with the lonely feelings that come with PIDS. Kenny said doing things like volunteering at events or manning water stations at training runs can help athletes keep the bonds they've made on their Ironman journeys.

After finishing the Ironman, some athletes have important stories to tell. Kyle and Brent Pease are among several athletes who have written books about their Ironman experiences. The brothers completed Ironman Wisconsin in 2013. Kyle has cerebral palsy and had grown up watching his brothers compete in sports. Kyle and Brent decided to take on the Ironman course together. They used the competition as a platform to create awareness for athletes with disabilities. Brent was with Kyle every step of the way. He pushed his brother through the water on a raft and led Kyle through the running portion in his wheelchair. And in 2018, the brothers got an opportunity to race in the World Championship in Kona.

The duo represented what the competition is about. Ironman triathlons are for all of those who want to test themselves. Some athletes have competed in the Olympics. Others took months out of their lives to train for one or two specific races. All that hard work and dedication builds up to one specific goal: the powerful feeling of crossing an Ironman finish line.

GLOSSARY

adrenaline
A substance released in the body of a person who is feeling a strong emotion such as excitement or fear.

amputee
A person who has lost all or part of a limb.

carbohydrate
One type of nutrient used to send energy to a person's body.

climate
The weather conditions of a specific area.

cramp
A tightening of muscles that causes pain, often due to dehydration.

currents
The movements of water.

electrolyte
A nutrient that helps to improve energy levels.

fatigue
Extreme tiredness.

immune system
A system in the body that protects the body from unwanted substances.

pace
The speed at which an athlete progresses through a race.

protein
A nutrient made up of amino acids that the body uses for energy.

terrain
The physical qualities of the land within a region.

MORE INFORMATION

BOOKS

Bright, Annie. *Hawaii*. Minneapolis, MN: Abdo Publishing, 2023.

Hanlon, Luke. *4 Deserts Ultramarathon Series*. Minneapolis, MN: Abdo Publishing, 2024.

Hewson, Anthony K. *Badwater 135*. Minneapolis, MN: Abdo Publishing, 2024.

ONLINE RESOURCES

To learn more about Ironman triathlons, please visit **abdobooklinks.com** or scan this QR code. These links are routinely monitored and updated to provide the most current information available.

INDEX

Brazil, 16

Carfrae, Mirinda, 4, 6–7
Collins, John, 8
Collins, Judy, 8

dehydration, 21–22
Denmark, 4
Diaper Dash, 17

Frankfurt, Germany, 22

hyponatremia, 22

Iden, Gustav, 24
Ironkids Fun Run, 17
Ironman Texas, 21
Ironman Wisconsin, 29

Kenny, Rogeema, 14, 26–28
Kona, Hawaii, 4, 7–9, 17, 29

Mission Bay Triathlon, 8
Moss, Julie, 21

Nice, France, 7, 17
Norway, 24

Oahu, Hawaii, 7

Pease, Brent, 29
Pease, Kyle, 29
post-Ironman depression syndrome (PIDS), 26–28

Rascon, Art, 21
Reinertsen, Sarah, 26
Ryf, Daniela, 4, 6

San Diego, California, 8
Sweden, 16
Switzerland, 4

Toddler Dot Trot, 17

ABOUT THE AUTHOR

Ethan Olson is a sportswriter and editor based in Minneapolis.